Introduction

Procrastination
    Procrastination Is Not Laziness
    Visualize the Future You Want
    Harness Fear by Turning it to Power
    Ways to Reward Yourself for Completing a Goal or Task

Personal Values
    Try This If You're Struggling to Find Your Passion
    Life Goals: Why You Should Be Setting Goals in Life
    Tools to Help Keep Track of Habits and Goals

Beautiful Thoughts
    Meditation 101: Techniques, Benefits, and a Beginner's How-to
    Embrace Positive Thinking
    Powerful Tips to Overcome Negative Thoughts
    How to Train your Brain to Kick the Worry Habit
    Everything is Important and Nothing is Important. Decide What's Unimportant to You

Conclusion

Introduction

Do you have the tendency to worry a lot, procrastinate, or constantly think that you won't get what you want? This is quite normal for people to think that way with all the challenges that life throws at us. While everyone feels these overwhelming feelings, it becomes a big problem when you experience these thoughts consistently. When this happens, you won't be able to function with your daily routines properly because you're always worried about the "what ifs" and the "what abouts". If you worry about things too much, you'll tend to procrastinate and lose your confidence to do things.

So, is there a way to change all of this and get a more positive outlook on life?

Fortunately, there is! You see, the brain is actually powered by our thoughts. If we fill our minds with negative thoughts, our actions will also be a reflection of those thoughts.

The wise Taoist Lao Tzu states, "Watch your thoughts; they become words. Watch your words; they become actions. Watch your actions; they become habit. Watch your habits; they become character. Watch your character; it becomes your destiny."

In essence, everything stems out from our thoughts. The more we think about negative things, the more we worry. The more we worry, the more we have the tendency to develop anxiety. If we develop anxiety, the more we will procrastinate. The more we procrastinate, the more we develop negative thoughts because we won't get anything done -- and the cycle continues and continues.

If we want to stop the cycle, then we simply have to reverse the process and constantly think of only positive thoughts. Of course, this is easier said than done, which is why we have developed a step by step guide to help you. In this book, you'll learn the fundamentals of creating beautiful thoughts, revamping your personal values, and dealing with procrastination. From there, you'll also learn how to build better relationships with the people around you and give your whole life a complete detox.

Let's get started!

Why We Need Mindfulness

Let's start by talking about mindfulness. In a general sense, mindfulness is a state of mind in which you are attentive to everything around you -- internally and externally.

Why is this concept important?

Often times, we manifest negative thoughts without us even knowing about it. Our subconscious brain can be influenced by the prevailing thoughts that our mind produces. This is why prevailing thoughts may actually turn into habits.

Imagine that you are filling your brain with negative thoughts. Since these negative thoughts will be embedded into your subconscious, you'll now think of negative thoughts automatically. The worst part is that you most likely won't be aware that you're manifesting negative thoughts because it has already become a habit. This is the exact reason why you'll need to be mindful. If you're in a state of mindfulness, you can observe every one of your thoughts and feelings from an objective point of view. Once you've faced them, you can clearly think of a way to eradicate them.

Procrastination

If there is one main enemy of goal setting, it is definitely procrastination. Procrastination is the act of delaying a certain action to a later time when you can actually do it now. What makes procrastination a hinder to your goals is that it delays them to a certain point where you won't try to reach your goals anymore. However, you don't need to worry because everyone has experienced procrastinating about something in their lives. Everyone has done it. Although it is quite a common thing to do, it is actually quite easy to fix. As long as you understand the concept of procrastination and the ways that it can affect your goals, you can kick out the habit.

Procrastination Is Not Laziness

In order to cure procrastination, you have to understand what procrastination is and what it's not. Contrary to what most people think, procrastination is not laziness. Yes, I would agree that there are some elements of laziness in procrastination, but they're not synonymous. In fact, you can actually be a workaholic but still procrastinate a lot.

So what exactly is procrastination?

Procrastination, in the dictionary definition, means always delaying a certain act or task no matter how urgent it is. With this meaning alone, we can't say that procrastination is laziness. Laziness is simply one of the effects of procrastination. If that is the case, then there should be other causes of procrastination, too. Here are a few common ones other than laziness:

- Fear

This is one of the most common reasons of procrastination. A lot of people procrastinate because they're scared of doing a certain task without really realizing it. For example, you're tasked to approach a random person to sell a condo unit. If you're a very shy person who doesn't like to talk to people you don't know, you'll probably procrastinate in your head and not end up doing the task. More often than not, people procrastinate because they're scared of doing the task.

- Lack of Motivation

Another reason could be lack of motivation. Sure, you're obligated to do something but are not really motivated to do it. If you don't have any motivation to do it, you'll most likely keep on putting it off until you end up not doing it at all.

- Priority Management

This is usually the reason why hardworking people procrastinate -- they have other things to do. Let's say that you're a freelance homebased worker working on many deadlines. Aside from your deadlines, you have other obligations as well such as housework. However, if you have a stream of deadlines from your work, you'll most likely keep on putting off or delaying your household chores until much later that you'll also end up not doing it. The main reason is because you prioritize your work and get so caught up in it that you'll not pay attention to other important tasks.

- Low Energy

The last reason is because of low energy. Some people confuse this with lacking motivation or simply with being lazy. Having low energy could be caused by a number of things from feeling a bit sick to just being sluggish.

Visualize the Future You Want

While you may have experienced all of these causes and have procrastinated a lot in the past, you have the chance to change it so you don't procrastinate anymore. The first step is to simply visualize the future you want. With this, we go back to goal setting. Once again, goal setting will allow you to set the direction for yourself so that you'll know where to go. If you want to stop procrastinating, you have to keep on reminding yourself of your destination. The best way to do it is with meditation. Here are a few steps on how to visualize your goal clearly and meditate on it.

Step 1: Choose a very quiet place where you won't be disturbed.

Step 2: Sit upright in a very comfortable position. Choose a nice chair with a back rest so you won't strain your back. If you want, you may also lie down on your bed or on your sofa.

Step 3: Start first by breathing in slowly a deep breath and breathing it out.

Step 4: Start by thinking about a goal that you'll want to achieve in three months. Now visualize what it will be like when you have already completed that goal. Take note that it must be a strong goal that is worth fighting for. Just visualize that for a few minutes.

Step 5: At first, you may be visualizing it from a third person point of view because that's usually more comfortable. However, after a while, visualize it from your point of view or from a first person point of view. This is usually more powerful.

Step 6: Lastly, power up that image by giving more energy into it. Then, after that, visualize dropping the image into your brain.

Harness Fear by Turning it to Power

Just now, we've established that one of the strongest reasons for procrastination is actually fear. Since it's one of the most powerful causes, let's tackle it and try to eradicate it.

The thing about fear is that it is so powerful that it can make you do (or not do) things without you really thinking. For example, if you're scared of spiders and you see one out of nowhere, your first reaction is to jump and flee. Same thing with doing tasks. If you're afraid to do a certain task, your first reaction will be to flee from it. Hence, procrastination comes in.

The best way to let go of fear is to convert it into power.

Let's apply some positive rules here and jazz it up a bit to fit the scenario. We talked about converting negative thoughts into positive thoughts. Using the same idea, let's see fear as a negative trait and empowerment as a positive one. You see, when we fear something, we think we are weak against it. However, when we feel strong against it, we are no longer afraid but empowered. Here are the steps to convert fear into power:

Step 1: List down all the fears that you have and also include what makes you fear those things.

Step 2: Once you've listed all of your fears, the next step is to weigh your options. What would happen if you faced your fear? For example, if you have a fear of public speaking, what will happen if you get on stage. List the pros and cons of your fears.

Step 3: Check out the fears that give you more pros than cons if you face them. Once you read them, you'll actually see how good it will be if you go against your initial fears.

Step 4: Continuously affirm yourself that you are powerful enough to face your fears. Just like what we did in the "Embrace Positive Thinking" section, we have to make sure that we always tell ourselves that we can do it.

Step 5: Lastly, act on it. While you are continuously affirming yourself that you can do it, you may refer back to your checklist so that you'll be reminded of all the benefits you'll get as compared to the cons. This will give you more motivation to do it.

Ways to Reward Yourself for Completing a Goal or Task

It's also good to reward yourself sometimes for a job well done. Once you've gotten over your procrastination and your fears, you'll be able to get your goals done faster. Of course, it's good to give yourself a nice pat in the back once you've accomplished a task that you've wanted to finish. No matter how driven you are to complete your goal, never forget to spend some time on yourself. It'll keep you happy and satisfied. Here are a few ways to reward yourself:

- Treat yourself to your favorite meal.
- Buy something that you've always wanted like a new phone, a new game, or a new book.
- Bring your loved ones or your significant other on a day out to join you in celebration of finishing your task.
- Go out on a date with yourself and enjoy the evening.
- Download or buy a new movie or series and binge watch.
- Simply just do anything that you want to do.

The way you celebrate will really depend on what you want. These are just suggestions that you may try out. Just make sure to always reward yourself for a job well done so that you can show yourself some appreciation.

Personal Values

Those are some of the steps that you do when you visualize and meditate on your goals. Do that for at least once a day and do step 6 five times during your session. If you do this every day, you'll eventually be filled with fiery passion every time you think of your goals. It will immediately push you to do it and prevent procrastination.

Try This If You're Struggling to Find Your Passion

In the last section, we talked about passion and how passion must be one of the values that we live by. It's important that we have a passion and a zest for life by doing things we're passionate about. If we don't, we'll just be getting that dragging feeling of floating through life every single day.

Now, what if you don't know what you're passionate about? Did you ever have a passion in life? Did you ever have a chance to develop a passion? If you currently don't have a passion, here are a few ways to help you find it:

Tip 1: Never Confuse Passion with Career

This is the first thing to always take note of -- your passion isn't necessarily your career. A lot of young people who are most likely just fresh out from college usually have their dreams crushed because they think that passion should be their career. More often than not, your passion may not end up to be your job because you need to prioritize paying your bills instead of thinking of your dreams. What if your passion doesn't make you enough money to pay your bills? This doesn't mean that you should give up your passion. It simply means that you have to work hard so that you can pursue your passion.

Tip 2: Keep on Trying New Things

If you haven't found your passion yet, just keep on trying. Never let go of your passion for learning new skills and things. Who knows? Your passion could just be there waiting to be learned. Always have the appetite for trying new things because it can bring you very far.

Tip 3: Don't Keep on Thinking About Money

Once again, your passion may not necessarily be your job, so you don't need to keep on thinking about how much money it can bring you. As long as it can bring you happiness and joy, it's good enough. If your passion happens to be your job, then that is very fortunate. If not though, just do it because it makes you happy. You can get a day job to give you the money.

Tip 4: Don't Limit Your Passion to Only One

A lot of people think that a passion is just one thing. However, this is a big mistake because it's possible to be passionate about many things. For example, your original passion was to draw portraits. Then, out of a sudden, you tried writing short stories which you also turned into a passion. Should you choose between the two? Is it really necessary to decide which one should be your one true passion? Absolutely not! As long as doing it makes you happy and fulfilled, then it is a passion. If you have two or more of those, then you can enjoy doing all of them whenever you want.

Tip 5: Don't Give Up

Never ever give up on your passion once you've found it. You may think that it doesn't fit into your schedule or it doesn't bring you money. However, none of that matters because it does its job of making you happy. As long as it makes you happy, put aside some time and some of your budget to do it simply because it'll make you feel good about yourself.

Life Goals: Why You Should Be Setting Goals in Life
──

Goal setting is one of the most important things to do in life because it enables you to look at what you want in the future. Here are some of the reasons why you should always set goals for yourself.

- You Can Get Direction

First of all, goal setting gives you direction in life. Notice that there are a lot of people who seem to just float by with their lives and seem dead every day. Even if they're working the hardest that they can, they can't seem to get that break. This is most probably because they don't get out of their comfort zones and they don't take the time to set goals. Setting goals means putting a standard for yourself and getting there. If you put a benchmark to how you should be in the future, you will have a direction to run to.

- You Can Get Focus

With direction, you can achieve total focus. Now, do take note that goal setting isn't just about wanting something or wanting to be someone -- that's just the first part. Goal setting is about setting a standard for yourself in the future and mapping out how you're going to do it. If you do this, you'll get focus on what you're supposed to do because you have a specific plan for your life. With a specific plan, you can get a laser-like focus that will allow you to achieve what you want.

- You Have Something to Fight For

There's a big difference between having obligations and having something to fight for. When you have obligations, you are forced to do something so that you can cover your obligations. Those aren't goals. Goals are destinations in life that you want to reach so that you can become happier. With goals, you are fighting for your happiness. You have something that you want to fight for. With this kind of mindset, you'll have a fiery passion that will enable you to do just about anything to reach that goal.

- You Are Forced to Act

If you have a very solid goal or goals, you will definitely be forced to act. Those who aren't forced to act upon their goals even if they have it either don't want it badly enough or don't know how to achieve it. This is why it was mentioned earlier that goal setting has to be as specific as possible. If you have a very general goal like "I want to be rich" without a "how", you can't exactly act on it. However, if you have a goal and a plan, you'll be forced to act. Otherwise, you know you'll never reach there.

- You Can Get Results

Lastly, you'll get the results you want. Most people who know how to set very specific goals in their lives get the results that they want. This is simply because they know exactly how to get them. The only thing left for these people to do is to act upon their plan. With the right goal setting skills, you can get the results you want. We'll go over some goal setting tools in the next section to help you make goals and keep track of them.

Tools to Help Keep Track of Habits and Goals

Goals aren't dreams that fall onto your lap because you want them to. Goals are specific plans that represent a certain standard that you want to achieve in your life. Think of your goals as plants. In order for your plant to bear fruit, you need to nurture them daily so that they don't die. As such, you'll need tools and materials such as soil, fertilizer, pots, water, mulch, and other things needed to help the plant grow. In the same way, goals need to be nurtured. You'll also need a number of tools to help you nurture your goals. Here are a few of my favorite tools that I use when setting and monitoring my goals and actions.

1. Daily Planner

Nothing really beats the classic daily planner. The daily planner has pretty much everything that you need for your goal setting. It has a section in the front that allows you to write down all your goals for the year. In the next section is the part that allows you to write down all the things that you need to do on a daily basis per date. This allows you to write down the general action that you need to do. This can be used to help you intelligently achieve your life goals.

1. Post-It Notes

Another thing to supplement your goals are post-it notes. The great thing about post-it notes is that they're visible. As long as you post them in places where you can always see them (like, let's say, your computer or work desk), you'll always be able to see them. Post-it notes are extremely powerful, and they can help remind you of the things that you want to achieve in the future.

- Dream Board

This is something that a lot of motivational speakers teach their students to do. A dream board is basically a large cut-out cardboard that contains pictures of all your life dreams. For example, it's your dream to travel the world and see the 7 Wonders someday. On your dream board, you'll put pictures of all the 7 Wonders. Then, you'll place your dream board in your room. With this, you'll wake up and see your dreams every day. This will give you a chance to be reminded about what you want. This is a powerful motivational tool that keeps people's fires burning.

- Goal Setting Apps

If you're not that keen on writing, then maybe you'd prefer goal setting apps instead. There are a lot of goal setting apps in App Stores. These apps are specifically built to help you have a platform to list down all of your goals and all of the steps that you need to take to reach your goals. One of the biggest advantages of apps like these is that they're right in your phone so you can monitor them anywhere you go as long as you have your phone with you.

- Goal Diary/Journal

These handy tools are diaries that allow you to list down your goals and write about them in a personal manner. Unlike the daily planner, goal diaries are not usually sectioned by date. In fact, a lot of goal diaries are creatively made with a lot of designs, illustrations, and pages that help you monitor your goals better.

Beautiful Thoughts

The only way you're going to eradicate negative thoughts is by simply replacing them with beautiful thoughts. How exactly do you do this? It's not like you can just pick out the negative thoughts and push the positive thoughts into your brain. There are certain techniques that you must use to do so. Let's discuss the techniques in this section.

Meditation 101: Techniques, Benefits, and a Beginner's How-to

Let's start with meditation. Most people associate meditation with relaxation because most stressed out people use this method as a way to calm themselves. While meditation does have a calming effect, it's much more than just that. Meditation is actually a way of cleaning your brain and reaching a higher level of mindfulness. Just to give you an idea, here are a few benefits you can have from meditation:

- Relaxed Disposition

First of all, meditation will help you relax, as what we've mentioned earlier. Meditation allows you to calm both the mind and the body by forcing you to think about absolutely nothing. This energizes the brain and makes you calm in general.

- Increased Amount of Grey Matter

Grey matter is responsible for your physical and emotional wellbeing. It regulates your muscle movement, senses, emotions, and your thoughts. Increasing grey matter in the brain will help you be able to control these aspects of your body better. Plus, increased grey matter can keep your brain from aging.

- Better Concentration

Another benefit meditation gives is concentration. As said above, meditation helps energize your brain. Because of this, you can hyper focus your thoughts and turn them into action subsequently. This allows you to stop procrastination as a whole.

- Sharper Brain

Believe it or not, meditation can make you smarter. It will rev up your brain and also help you focus (as we mentioned above).

- Clearer Perspective

Finally, you will have a clearer perspective of life. One of the great things about meditation is that it brings your mind to a higher plane of consciousness—higher than even your physical body. With this, you can actually view things from a third party point of view, gaining you more insight and giving you more mindfulness.

Now that you pretty much know the benefits meditation can give you, let's go on to the meditation 101 guide. Before we go to techniques, it's very important to first know the basic principle behind meditation.

The basic idea of meditation is focus.

Yes! It's as simple as that. Meditation is all about fixating your focus into a single entity so that your mind will not think about anything else. For most basic meditation practices, teachers will teach students to fixate on their breathing, which is what we will put emphasis on.

Before you meditate, I suggest that you prepare three very important things:

- A nice and quiet place in your home with no distractions
- A comfortable place to sit on
- A timer (you can use a meditation app that provides relaxing alarms)

Once you have these three things, you're ready for meditation. Simply follow this step-by-step process:

Step 1: Go to your place of relaxation. Make sure that there are no distractions and no noise. You need absolute peace and quiet to start.

Step 2: Get a meditation chair or a meditation cushion. If you easily have backaches, I suggest that you start out with a meditation chair so that you have something to lean on. After that, sit down on your chair (if you have enough space, you can cross your legs but if not, you can sit normally) and make sure that your back is straight.

Step 3: Once you're in a very relaxed position, start your timer and set a very calm and quiet alarm. For beginners, I suggest 10 minutes per day. You can increase the duration once you get the hang of it. From there, put your timer aside, close your eyes and put your hands on your lap.

Step 4: Inhale deeply and slowly through your nose while simultaneously expanding your stomach. After that, exhale slowly also through your nose while simultaneously deflating your stomach. This is the type of breathing that you should do.

Step 5: Continue your slow breathing and deeply put your focus on it. If you can hear yourself breathing, that means you're doing it correctly. Feel the air as it enters your nose and fills up your lungs. After that, feel the air go out of your lungs and exit your nose.

Step 6: While you're doing this, you might be tempted to think of something like a proposal that you have to do or a deadline that you have to complete tomorrow. Sure, it's tempting to think about everything that you have to do, but slowly shift your attention back to your breathing. Tell yourself that you have to go back to your breathing. Keep doing so until your timer sounds.

Step 7: If you're still having a hard time concentrating, you can count your breaths. This is a very useful technique that will allow you to zoom in on your breathing.

Step 8: Finally, increase the amount of time that you meditate. You may start off with 10 minutes per day for about a week or two. However, as you go along, you may try to increase to 20 minutes or 30 minutes. Do remember that this cannot be done overnight because meditation isn't something that you rush. Casually increase the number of minutes based on your own capacity.

These are the 8 steps to basic meditation. Now, you may be frustrated at first because your mind might be too restless or that you can't seem to get comfortable. Believe me, this is a very normal thing to experience. However, as long as you consistently practice, you'll be able to get it. Meditation is an art that takes time to perfect. Start out small and you'll perfect your technique in no time.

Embrace Positive Thinking

You're probably familiar with positive thinking from movies or from positivity preachers on TV. While there are a lot of people who might be skeptical about positive thinking, it is actually proven to work. Positive thinking is the art of feeding your brain with positive thoughts so that it can manifest into actions and habits.

In the previous section, we've learned about meditation. With meditation, our brain will be in a more relaxed and mindful state helping us to fully be aware of our own thoughts. The next step to replacing negative thoughts with positive thoughts is to push more positive thoughts into our heads.

For those who are new to this concept, what exactly is positive thinking?

You may think that positive thinking is just trying to be positive while hiding away from all your troubles. No, positive thinking is not trying to be happy despite all your challenges in life. This is known as false positivity. Positive thinking is about embracing life's most challenging situations and still maintaining a positive outlook.

So how exactly do you start with positive thinking? I've broken it down into a few simple steps that you can follow:

Step 1: The first thing to do is determine the areas in your life that you usually think negatively about. These areas are known as areas of change because you want to change them.

Step 2: Take note of all your negative thoughts without the day and write them down. Once you make your list, try to give them a more positive spin by rephrasing them.

Step 3: Let go of all the toxic people in your life. There's a saying that goes, "Tell me who your friends are and I'll tell you who you are." If you have friends that are full of negativity, the tendency is you'll also harbor some negative thoughts as well. So in order for you to completely let go of those negative thoughts, let go of those people too.

Step 4: Start affirming yourself from the start of the day to the end. This is proactive self-talk that will allow you to feed and embed your mind with good thoughts. You can start out with simple "I'm feeling good" statements. After that, you can identify the areas of change and start turning your existing negative thoughts into positive ones. For example, if you have a bad boss, instead of thinking, "I don't like him because he's a bad boss." Try to change it to, "I can do anything he throws at me."

Powerful Tips to Overcome Negative Thoughts

Negative thoughts may come without warning. They're not always just embedded in your head and manifesting every now and then. In fact, we sometimes experience negative thoughts on a daily basis out of nowhere. For example, if you create a blunder at work and take it badly, you'll harbor negative thoughts all day. So to further help you dispel any negative thoughts, here are a few powerful tips you can use.

Tip 1: Look at the Lesson

Every failure has a lesson attached to it. Looking at the lesson will not only force you to dispel the negative emotions of failure or adversity but also give you more insights for improvement.

Tip 2: Don't Think about What Others Think

This is one of the hardest things to do. Often times, we get worried about what other people think about us and miss out a lot of opportunities in the process. In order not to do so, practice not caring about what other people have to say about you.

Tip 3: Positive Thinking

As we have already mentioned in the previous section, positive thinking is extremely powerful and it can help replace negative emotions. What you can do is create a positive mantra that you can repeat to yourself over and over if something bad happens to you. It can be somewhere along the lines of, "I can do anything if I put my mind to it" or "I will not be affected by any adversity".

Tip 4: Rant to a Friend

The worst thing that one can do during an adversity is to keep everything in. You see, the more you keep those emotions in, the more you'll harbor negative thoughts. It's better to rant to a friend and get it off your chest than keeping it in.

Tip 5: Work Out

Finally, you can try to work out a bit. Exercise helps release endorphins which is a type of happy hormone that can help you cope with problems better because they can give a sort of euphoric high. So if you're too stressed or troubled, a short work out can be very helpful.

How to Train your Brain to Kick the Worry Habit

Worrying is something that a lot of people do on a daily basis simply because life itself is very uncertain. With uncertainty comes discomfort and with discomfort comes worry. Who wouldn't worry about something like a ton of bills to pay in the coming month? Who wouldn't worry about an ongoing condition that may affect the future? Or who wouldn't worry about when the next hurricane will hit?

Yes, there are definitely so many things to worry about. However, it's not really the worrying that we should be concerned about. It's our reaction to worrying that we should take heed. After we worry about something, what's next? Do we brood over it or do we do something about it? If you chose the former, then it will most likely result in a lot of anxiety and negative thoughts.

Fortunately, there are techniques that we can use to kick off the worry habit and start living again. No longer will you have to be a slave of your worries if you know how to kick them out. With that said, here are some very effective tips on how to train your brain to get rid of all your worry habits:

Step 1: Determine the Source of Your Worries

It may be your job, your bills, your parents, the weather, or diseases. Make a list of the things that scare you and ask yourself what you can do about them. There are certain things in our life that we can control and yet there are also certain things in our life that we can't. In order to change our mindset, we have to first identify the source of fears and label them as controllable or uncontrollable.

Step 2: Create Solutions to Those Worries

Let's first discuss the things that we can control. Let's say that you have a pile of bills to pay but with little money to pay for them. Money is something that you can control because you bring in your own income. Two possible solutions to this problem is to either cut back on your expenses or get another source of income. By creating logical solutions to these controllable situations, you lessen your worries and get things done.

Step 3: Think of What to Do for Things You Can't Control

Things such as other people, the weather, and illnesses cannot be controlled. For this, the only thing that can be controlled is your reactions and actions. Let's say you have a rather unreasonable boss at work who chews on you all the time. You can't tell your boss to stop being angry all the time because it most probably won't work. The best thing you can do is to either quit your job, don't mind him/her, or try to please him/her. However, if you take it personally and start to feel bad, you'll start feeling a whole set of worries about whether or not your boss will chew you off tomorrow or the next day. For worries that you can't control, you may just think of a counter-measure to help you cope with it.

Everything is Important and Nothing is Important. Decide What's Unimportant to You

More often than not, people tend to think of too many things-- even things that aren't really important. This in itself can already create a lot of negative thoughts and anxiety. Just imagine, cramming too many things into your mind at a single time can make it breakdown. This is why a lot of people suffer nervous breakdowns. This is why you need to declutter your minds from time to time.

Conclusion

In order to declutter your mind, you have to first determine what are the things that are really important to you. For example, you're always with a friend who happens to be toxic and is negatively affecting you. Ask yourself why are you with this person all the time. Is it because you genuinely enjoy his/her company? Or is it because you feel pity for him/her or don't have anyone else to be with? If it's the latter, then your friend really has no place in your mind. In that instance, it's better to just stop being with him/her too often because his/her toxic disposition negatively affects you.

While you have your alone time, always try to evaluate what are the things important in your life. Those things that are not important, cut them out because they won't do you any good. This will give you a more positive outlook on life and reduce anything negative.

www.ingramcontent.com/pod-product-compliance
Lightning Source LLC
Chambersburg PA
CBHW030058230526
45471CB00003B/1154